Forbidden Fruit

T0015557

Forbidden Fruit

An Anthropologist Looks at Incest

Maurice Godelier

Translated by Nora Scott

VERSO

London • New York

This work was translated with the financial aid of CREDO – Centre de Recherche et de Documentation sur l'Océanie.

This English-language edition first published by Verso 2023
Translation © Nora Scott 2023
First published as *L'Interdit de l'inceste à travers les sociétés*
© CNRS Éditions 2021

1 3 5 7 9 10 8 6 4 2

Verso
UK: 6 Meard Street, London W1F 0EG
US: 388 Atlantic Avenue, Brooklyn, NY 11217
versobooks.com

Verso is the imprint of New Left Books

ISBN-13: 978-1-80429-234-1
ISBN-13: 978-1-80429-235-8 (UK EBK)
ISBN-13: 978-1-80429-236-5 (US EBK)

British Library Cataloguing in Publication Data
A catalogue record for this book is available from the British Library

Library of Congress Cataloging-in-Publication Data

Names: Godelier, Maurice, author. | Scott, Nora, translator.
Title: Forbidden fruit : an anthropologist looks at incest / Maurice
    Godelier ; Translated by Nora Scott.
Other titles: L'interdit de l'inceste à travers les sociétés. English
Description: London ; New York : Verso, 2023. | "First published as
    L'Interdit de l'inceste à travers les sociétés © CNRS Editions 2021"
    — Title page verso. | Includes bibliographical references.
Identifiers: LCCN 2023013751 (print) | LCCN 2023013752 (ebook) | ISBN
    9781804292341 (trade paperback) | ISBN 9781804292365 (ebook)
Subjects: LCSH: Incest. | Sex—Anthropological aspects.
Classification: LCC GN480.25 .G64 2023 (print) | LCC GN480.25 (ebook) |
    DDC 320.53223—dc24/eng/20230105
LC record available at https://lccn.loc.gov/2023013751
LC ebook record available at https://lccn.loc.gov/2023013752

Typeset in Sabon by Biblichor Ltd, Scotland
Printed and bound by CPI Group (UK) Ltd, Croydon CR0 4YY

For Lina

Contents

If we were unaware of the Egyptian custom of brothers marrying their sisters, we would wrongly assert that it is universal knowledge that a man cannot marry his sister.

Sextus Empiricus
Greek philosopher and physician
Second century CE

Foreword

I feel I need to provide the readers of this little book with some of the background surrounding its birth. During the summer of 2020, I was in Greece, on the island of Andros, trying to finish a book on the question 'Is it possible to become a modern society without becoming Westernized?' I had promised CNRS Éditions it would be done before the end of the year. But my health took a turn for the worse: I became unable to walk and was finally transported to a clinic in Athens.

Before this, however, I had followed the debates on French television sparked by the publication of Camille Kouchner's book, *La Familia grande*, which discreetly evokes a case of homosexual incest committed by a stepfather on his stepson. I had followed a series of interesting television programmes featuring psychologists and sociologists discussing incest, but I was sorry to see that no anthropologists had been invited, although it is our profession to analyse relationships and kinship systems, and to identify the role played in societies by the taboo on incest. So, I called Anne Chemin, who writes in the French daily *Le Monde*, with whom I had already worked, to let her know how I felt. Anne Chemin responded with an invitation from the paper's editors to make a contribution on this subject.

Anne Chemin and I had begun to draw up some questions even before my hospitalization. As soon as I was able to leave the clinic, I felt driven to revisit these questions and to find some answers. So, from my bed – without benefit of books or notes – I dictated my questions and answers to my assistant, Anne-Sylvie Malbrancke. The dictated version went back and forth between Anne Chemin and myself, and ultimately appeared in the 27 March 2021 issue of *Le Monde*. That was when Blandine Genthon, head of CNRS Éditions, asked me if I had more to say on the subject. Of course, I said that I had only just begun and still had a lot more to say.

CNRS Éditions suggested I continue and turn the article into a small book. Still obliged to rely on the virtual library in my head, I therefore had to stick to essentials.

The reader will easily understand how grateful I am to everyone who helped me, in somewhat difficult circumstances, carry out this project, and I thank them warmly here.

Athens, 15 April 2021

Chapter 1
The Incest Taboo

Can you define what constitutes incest?

To go directly to the heart of the definition, I would say that, beyond the many forms it takes in different cultures, the term 'incest' designates the prohibition on parents having sexual relations with their children and on brothers and sisters having sexual relations with each other. But we need to be careful here: in many societies, depending on the nature of the kinship system (including among the Dravidian or Iroquois, for example), all of the father's brothers are as fathers for the child, all of the mother's sisters are as mothers of the child, and all of their children are as brothers and sisters of the child. In these societies, the prohibition on incest therefore extends to all of those persons that in the West we regard as uncles, aunts or first cousins. But it must be remembered that whereas my father's brothers are also my fathers, they are, nevertheless, not my mother's husbands and do not have sexual relations with her.

These systems show that societies differentiate between parenthood as a social relation, which can extend to many people, and father and mother as a physical, bodily relation, which concerns only two people, whom in the West we call biological parents. Until the end of the nineteenth century, human societies were unaware of the real biological process involved in conceiving a child. Faced with this mystery and before the advent of modern science, they invented myths about how babies were made. If we are to understand the variety of forms of incest, it is crucial to know about these social imaginaries, for it was using these collective beliefs that societies crafted prohibitions on certain sexual practices.

No society considers sexual relations between a man and a woman to be sufficient to make a child. I arrived at this conclusion after comparing the beliefs of dozens of societies. What the couple makes is a foetus, but, in all cultures, the child is completed in the woman's womb by the arrival of a life force or principle, a spirit or an ancestor which imparts life to the foetal body and transforms it into a child. In Hinduism and Buddhism, the individual is the reincarnation of another person and will be reincarnated in yet another. In the

Christian religion, the soul that will impart life to a child's body is not made by the parents' sexual relations but is introduced into the woman by God when he so wishes and in the form he wishes. We can thank Hildegard of Bingen, a German nun living at the end of the twelfth century, for a painting showing a soul in the shape of a fireball entering the body of a pregnant woman.

In *The Metamorphoses of Kinship* (Verso, 2020), you write that the incest taboo is based on the fact that certain individuals are too 'alike'. What do you mean?

If incest is forbidden in all human societies, it is because it brings together persons that are considered to be 'too alike': they share essential components of their being, whether these be physical – sperm, blood, milk or flesh – or immaterial – the soul or the name. Bringing these components into contact through sexual intercourse is forbidden because this excess of sameness can be detrimental to them and those close to them, but it can also be detrimental to the reproduction of the social order as a whole and even the universe.

Is incest a universal taboo?

All human societies prohibit incest, but this universal taboo takes very different forms. Each culture determines the shared component that founds this prohibition: the notion I talked about – 'same/different' – varies from one society to the next. The ancient Egyptians thought that the union of a brother and sister posed no threat of a cosmic or social catastrophe, whereas in Western societies, this union is among those considered to be the most gravely incestuous.

In matrilineal kinship systems, in Africa, Oceania or among certain Amerindian groups, children belong to the maternal clan, in other words, to the mother's and her brother's clan. The mother's brother has authority over his sister's children and transmits his goods and titles to them. Trobriand Islanders, with whom the anthropologist Bronisław Malinowski lived at the beginning of the twentieth century, consider that a child is conceived when the spirit of an ancestor wants to be reborn in the body of one of his clan descendants. The foetus is the result of the mixing of the ancestor spirit and the woman's menstrual blood. The man's sperm therefore has nothing to do with engendering the child: the father, that is to say, the mother's husband, is not considered to be the genitor.

In this society, the worst crime, therefore, is for a mother to have sexual relations with her son, because he shares his identity with her and her ancestors. The fact that this incest is designated by a specific term (*suva-sova*) shows that this forbidden relationship is both thinkable and possible. For the same reason, it is also a crime for the mother's brother to have sexual relations with his niece. By contrast, sexual relations between father and daughter are not considered to be incestuous: in acting this way, the father makes bad social use of his penis, but he can, ultimately, have sexual relations with his daughter because he did not beget her.

For Western societies, what is socially and culturally negative about sexual relations between parent and child?

In the West, the family is a nuclear family: a man, a woman and their children. From the standpoint of sociology and affects, if a parent seduces and has sexual relations with their child, they set the child up as a rival of their spouse. These forbidden sexual relations destroy the authority of the older generations over the younger, which is necessary for the child's upbringing, well-being and morality. Incest endangers the basic sociological and psychological underpinnings of the family: it destroys the responsibility, authority and protection the members owe each other in order for their social ties to be sustained and socially and personally positive. Religions usually promise punishment for these transgressions, which extends beyond death.

To legitimize the prohibition of sexual relations between parents and children and between brothers and sisters, Christian theology invokes the dogma of *una caro*, which stipulates that when a man and a woman unite sexually, they become one flesh, and their children are the flesh of their flesh. What role has this dogma played in the prohibition of incest in the West?

In Western societies, Christianity has moulded sexual practices and prohibitions for the last 2,000 years. To understand the representations of incest that began to spread with the Middle Ages, we need to evoke a principle that the Bible traces back to Adam and Eve: when a man and a woman, married or not, unite sexually, they form one body, and this body is also that of their children: this is known as the dogma of *una caro*. In Genesis 2: 23–24, we read that Eve was created from Adam's body. When Adam sees Eve, he exclaims:

'"This at last is bone from my bones, and flesh from my flesh ..." This is why a man leaves his father and mother and joins himself to his wife, and they become one body' (The Jerusalem Bible).

This thesis – according to which Eve, the first woman, was born from a piece of Adam's body, so that they were, therefore, one flesh – would pose a few problems for Christian theologians. In the fourth century CE, in his book *The City of God*, Saint Augustine (354–430) acknowledged that the notion of *una caro* led to the conclusion that all humans descend from a series of incests: that between Adam and Eve after having been driven from Paradise, and then that of their children and their children's children. He writes:

> After the first sexual union between the man, created from dust, and the woman, created from the man's side, the human race needed, for its reproduction and increase, the conjunction of males and females, and the only human beings in existence were those from those two parents. Therefore, men took their sisters as wives. This was, of course, a completely decent procedure under the pressure of necessity; it became as completely reprehensible in later times, when it was forbidden by religion.

> Book XV, ch. 16, p. 623

He goes on to say, 'as soon as there came to be a supply of possible wives, who were not already their sisters . . . no longer was there a necessity for unions between brother and sister; such unions henceforth were banned' (p. 624). This was for the greater happiness of humankind, for 'affection was given its right importance so that men . . . should be bound together by ties of various relationships . . . and in that way they should help bind social life more effectively by involving in their plurality a plurality of persons' (p. 623).

Sixteen centuries later, Claude Lévi-Strauss would say much the same thing when praising the social advantages of exogamy and the multiplication of alliances. Saint Augustine knew full well that the ancient fathers did not like to marry half-sisters or full sisters, but they certainly liked to marry wives from their own family, and that, in the surrounding tribes, men continued to marry close cousins. He condemns this union in the name of decency, which ensures that 'kinship gives a woman a claim to honour and respect, she is shielded from the lust which, as we know, brings blushes even to the chastity of marriage' (p. 625).

Sexual desire, as a source of sin, is therefore excluded by the church. The only acceptable use of sex is for reproduction, without desire. The fate of sexual desire in Western society was thus sealed. On the other hand, the sacred texts of ancient India prescribe that a wife should pleasure her husband in all ways (*cf.* the *Kama Sutra*, which proposes positions for bringing sexual pleasure to both partners).

Does the Koran prohibit incest?

It is useful to compare the incests prohibited by Christian theology with those listed by the Prophet, which feature in the chapter of the Koran devoted to the woman (Chapter 4, verse 24).

> You are forbidden to marry your mothers, daughters, sisters, paternal aunts, maternal aunts, nieces, your foster-mothers, your foster-sisters, your mothers-in-law, your step-daughters whom you have brought up and with whose mothers you have had carnal relations. It would not be a sin to marry her if you did not have carnal relations with her mother. You are forbidden to marry the wives of your own sons and to marry two sisters at the same time without any adverse effect to such relations of the past.

These prohibitions are deserving of a long commentary, but, here, I will merely underscore several important points. As we see, the Prophet extends the prohibition on sexual relations to foster-mothers and children. A man shares a substance with his foster-sister – her mother's milk, which makes her as his own mother. Both the mother and the daughter are forbidden to him. It is important to note that any daughters born of a woman's first marriage are forbidden to her second husband. For the Prophet, these 'stepdaughters' are as daughters. The kin tie in this case is not based on a shared component; it is a social kin tie. Finally, Mohammed is fully aware that the Bedouins sometimes marry two sisters, as was also the case among the Jewish tribes – the Bible tells that Jacob married two sisters.

The prohibitions listed in the Koran are, in large part, the same as those stipulated in the Torah, in addition to the prohibitions on foster-kin and those on 'stepdaughters'. The Prophet also evokes God to legitimize men's domination of women (2: 34).

As in Saint Augustine, all of these prohibitions are defined from a male standpoint, a male ego. And this tradition continues today. It should also be noted that the Prophet had no need to invoke the metaphysical fantasy of *una caro* in drawing up his list. Which means that, in his time, these prohibitions were obvious for society, and so there was no need to invoke supernatural reasons to legitimize them.

On the other hand, the Christian dogma of *una caro* would considerably expand the definition of incest, wouldn't it?

Indeed, if husband and wife form one and the same body, and if this is also the case for parents and children, then the sister-in-law is as a sister, the brother-in-law is as a brother, the father-in-law as a father, the mother-in-law as a mother, while first cousins are as siblings and so on. By transforming affines into quasi-consanguines, Christian mythology expanded the circle of incest like concentric ripples in a pond. By the thirteenth century, the prohibition extended to cousins of the seventh degree – which the Catholic Church reduced to four and then two degrees over the following centuries. It must be remembered that, until the twelfth century, marriage, in Catholic Europe, was not a sacrament but an alliance between families; only later did it become a sacrament, celebrated before God in church, and therefore an unbreakable bond with no possibility of divorce, unless the union had not been consummated. This is not the case in the Orthodox Church, which authorizes divorces and the possibility of three marriages, or in the Protestant churches.

Let me add that in many societies, saying to a man that when he has sexual relations with a woman, he becomes the body of this woman, will cause him to vomit at the very idea of identifying with a woman, who is a source of impurity.

Is the condemnation of sexual relations between brother and sister as universal as the condemnation of sexual relations between parent and child?

It is almost universal. But there are some rare exceptions, which are deeply meaningful. In certain societies – Ancient Persia, Ancient Egypt or the Inca Empire, for instance – sexual relations between parent and child were strictly forbidden, but the union of a brother and a sister was, on the contrary, the most socially and religiously valued form of marriage.

However, if the taboo was lifted within the sibling generation, it was for religious reasons. According to the imaginary of the Mazdean state religion of Persia, humanity was born of a threefold incest among the gods: first between the god of Heaven and his daughter Earth; and then between their son and his mother, who bore twins; and then between this brother-and-sister pair, who were the ancestors of all humans – these twins embodied the perfect combination of male and female powers.

In this society, a few individuals were also called to unite with their sister in a particular rite (*xwêtôdas*) celebrated by a Mazdean priest who had married his own sister. This union was, therefore, experienced not as being incestuous but as the replication, by humans, of a divine act: it promoted Good and repelled Evil in the universe as well as in the society. Individuals married according to this rite were promised a prime place in Paradise. In these societies, the union of a brother with a sister was a way of sublimating incest as a mystical act that gave humans an active part in the divine world.

In _Totem and Taboo_ (1913), the founder of psychoanalysis, Sigmund Freud, wrote that the incest taboo emerged following the 'killing of the father', an event that he believed really to have happened in a remote pre-historical past. What do you think about this theory?

Freud, who observed that incestuous desires engender destructive rivalries within families, proposed a fictional account of the birth of human society. Summarizing Freud's text: at the outset, there was no society; there were consanguineous families composed of a man who had found a woman to unite with. They had children, and, when the girls reached puberty, the father kept them for himself. The frustrated sons decided to kill the father in order to take their mother and sisters for themselves, then they ate the father. Having murdered their father, the sons discovered that they were about to kill each other in order to fulfil their desires. And, so, they decided to exchange their own sisters for the sisters of other family groups. This, according to Freud, was how society was born from the exchange of women.

Archaeology and palaeoanthropology have completely discredited this scenario, which implies that the family existed before the emergence of society. But we know that humans are a naturally social species, which was originally organized in societies of hunter-gatherer-fishers. In these societies, families appeared when the sexual division of tasks – something that does not exist among the higher primates such as chimpanzees and bonobos – gave rise to cooperation between men and women in order to survive, and to feed and protect their children from the time of birth. So that is the origin of human families. In this process, the prohibition of incest never involved killing the fathers. The major social fact that needs to be stressed here is that the prohibition of incest is a founding, and therefore a constituent, component of all kinship relations.

Chapter 2
The Taboo on Incest
in Kinship Systems

You say that, in all societies, kinship relations create different systems and engender kin groups that fit these situations. What are these systems and what is the role of incest in their emergence and the way they work?

Before enumerating the kinship systems anthropology has discovered since the mid-nineteenth century, I will first discuss what all these systems have in common. Indeed, when we compare these systems, we discover that all rest on the active presence and interaction of six components, which are the basic building blocks of all kinship systems, their shared matrix, as it were. These components are interdependent and necessary, and therefore their relations are circular: each component implies the others and refers to them. These components are:

1 The descent principles, which are the rules that define the kin group or groups in society to which a child belongs from birth.

2 The incest taboo, defined by each society, which entails the prohibition of sexual relations and marriage with those persons considered by this society to be too like oneself.

3 Those rules regulating alliances by marriage or by other possible forms of union in the society under consideration.

4 The rules defining a newly formed couple's place of residence.

5 The ways each society represents the process of child conception in the context of its kinship system. These representations, in turn, determine the socially defined role ascribed to the man, the woman and eventually to other actors – ancestors, spirits, gods – in engendering and bringing a child into the world.

6 Kinship terms. Every society has its own specific vocabulary to designate kinship relations and positions (father, mother, cousins and so on) as defined by this society's kinship system.

Can you elaborate on the concrete nature of each of these components and their variants?

In effect, each of these components has several variants, but their number is always limited. Let us take the first component, for example: *descent*. In all societies, a child is the son or the daughter of a father and a mother; but for many societies, descent and filiation are distinct realities. Filiation designates those ties connecting children with their paternal kin (agnates) and their maternal kin (uterines). Filiation is always bilateral, and therefore cognatic: that is, it concerns both the agnatic and the uterine kin of a child. The child is indeed the son or daughter of a man and a woman, then, but it is often considered to descend uniquely from its father, from its father's father and so on; or, on the contrary, to descend uniquely from its mother, its mother's mother, etcetera.

The concrete application of these principles means that the child belongs exclusively to its father's clan in one case (patrilineal systems) or uniquely to its mother's clan in another (matrilineal systems). In the first case, the child will be under its father's authority, and in the second, under that of its mother's brother, its maternal uncle.

Societies with patrilineal kinship systems include the Bedouins, the Turks and the Baruya of New Guinea; those with matrilineal systems include the North American Iroquois, the Trobriand Islanders of New

Guinea, the Ashanti of Ghana and the Na of China. It is important to point out from the start that descent principles are imaginary norms, but they entail important social and material consequences. For instance, Trobriander society explains that humans first appeared in the form of brother–sister couples, and that subsequent humans descended only from the female ancestor. The result is that the blood flowing in the veins of these men and woman is female blood alone; the word for blood, *dala*, is also the word for the matrilineal clan. This shows us that descent principles are cultural constructions designed to organize the life of the society and are constructed using biological materials.

How many different ways of organizing an individual's ascendants and descendants are there?

To date, we have found four.

The first is the one we have just described: descent reckoning built on a unilineal principle, which goes through the men or through the women, thus giving rise to patrilineal or matrilineal kinship systems and groups.

The second formula is that of ambilineal systems: a child belongs to both its father's and its mother's clans, but receives different things from each clan; for instance, its name and land will come from the father, while religious and political functions will come from the mother. We find these systems in Africa, in the Congo, as well as in South India, but they are rare.

The third formula takes in bilineal systems, of which there are two kinds. In one, all of the sons belong to the father's clan and all of the daughters to the mother's clan (parallel bilineal systems). Rarer are those systems in which it is the daughters who belong to the father's clan and the sons to the mother's (cross bilineal). Such systems are found mainly in Oceania, in particular in New Guinea (Mundugumor – present-day Biwat, cross bilineal; Orokolo, parallel bilineal).

Finally, the fourth formula is that of non-lineal systems, also known as undifferentiated, in which a child belongs to both the father's and the mother's families as well as to those of its four grandparents. In these societies, there are no clans or lineages, but there are sometimes lines that run through the male line or more rarely through the female, and which can break down and disappear in any generation. In these systems, each individual that is born thus finds itself in an open group of kin and affines who are closely or more distantly related; this ego-centred group comprises its kindred. This is the form of descent found in most societies of Western Europe and North America, which are characterized by the nuclear family, but where children usually carry the father's name, giving greater weight to the paternal family.

Is this last formula restricted to Europe and America?

No. It is also found among the Inuit, who in the past had no historical or geographical contact with the West. This shows that the same kinship system can arise several times in different places over the course of human history. It is also found in Indonesia (among the Iban) and throughout Polynesia and Madagascar, as well as in Ancient Greece, with the demes created in Athens after Cleisthenes' reforms.

What role does the incest taboo play in the functioning of kinship systems?

Prohibition of incest constitutes the necessary bond between descent and alliance, which are the two fundamental pillars of kinship. As we have seen over its multi-millennial history, humankind has discovered by experience the negative impact on the reproduction of families and society as a whole of sexual unions with persons considered to be too like oneself, and consequently has forbidden them. But when it forbade such sexual relations, humankind, at the same time, created the obligation to look elsewhere for the partners needed to reproduce families.

The incest taboo is thus, at one and the same time, a prohibition and a prescription: the instruction to take partners outside one's group in order to continue to exist. The prohibition thus entails immediately the appearance of the third component of any kinship system: the obligation to answer the question 'Whom can I or can I not marry?'

But it must be stressed that the incest taboo extends to homosexual relations as well, even though they do not directly call into question the society's reproduction. It is also important to underscore that an anthropologist cannot know in advance, for a given society, what component, when shared by two individuals, would lead them to commit, in their own eyes, incest should they unite sexually. In some societies this component is the blood, in others, the bones, or the flesh or maternal milk – and even the breath.

For instance, in Ancient China, under the Chu dynasty (770–223 BCE), society was governed by a warrior nobility organized into large patrilineal clans (*tsu*); these clans contained all descendants of a common ancestor with whom they claimed to share not the same blood, but the same breath (*chi*). This breath united them in one community that connected them with their deceased ancestors, from whom they were never separated since it was always the same breath that animated a father and his sons down through the generations. The ancient Chinese notion of a community of breath thus had no ideological relation with that of a community of blood (*consanguinitas*), which we in the West inherited from Rome. And yet, the basic structures of the two kinship systems belong to the same type.

What are the principles governing alliances and therefore the various forms of marriage?

First, a remark: marriage is by no means a universal institution. In many societies, the union of a man and a woman to make a family does not entail a wedding ceremony. All that is needed is that no one oppose the union, on either the man's or the woman's side, and that their union respect local customs when it is made public. In contemporary French society, there are several forms of union: some people get married, some opt for co-habitation, others form common-law couples, and yet others establish a civil covenant, or PACS. It is peculiar to France that the state imposes on those who have a church wedding that they first of all go through a civil marriage and therefore are married in the eyes of the state. In Greece, on the other hand, where the Orthodox Church is the state religion, the religious marriage has the same civil status as the town hall marriage, which is not obligatory.

The types of union in the various societies fall into three forms:

1 union within own group, between non-forbidden close relatives;
2 union outside own group with more or less distant partners; and
3 union at once with own group and with outside groups.

What do you mean by 'union within one's own group'?

For example, in the Koran, the Prophet wanted to reduce the number of wives Bedouins were allowed to four. The first, and in the Prophet's eyes preferential, marriage was that of a man with his father's brother's daughter, in other words, a woman from his father's own clan. Taking a wife from this clan meant not having to pay a dowry to establish the union. On the other hand, this close female relative is forbidden in the Western Christian system of kinship.

What about union outside one's own group?

In very many societies, clans or lineages, when they exist, contract alliances and marry by exchanging women, in the majority of cases, but also in rare cases men.

The Baruya of New Guinea, for example, exchange women between clans, an exchange known as *ginamaré*. Sometime around the age of twenty, young Baruya men must leave the men's house where they have lived since their first-stage initiation around the age of ten or so. They leave this house to enter into a marriage agreed several years earlier, following the negotiation of their clan members to exchange one of the young man's sisters for one of another clan's girls, who is to become his wife. The young people are not consulted because their marriage is a matter for the lineages as a collective body, and not for their individual members. It is almost impossible for individuals to contest this decision, and their feelings are never the starting point for these alliances.

The alliance between lineages thus takes the form of the gift and reciprocal counter-gift of women between two kin groups, A and B. The nature of these reciprocal gifts is sometimes hard for Westerners to understand, for the counter-gift of a woman does not cancel the debt incurred by receiving a woman. The counter-gift does not mean giving back, then, but giving in turn. If giving implies that the giver is superior to the taker, then when A gives a woman to B, A is superior. But when B in turn gives a woman to A, B becomes superior as well. In the end, A and B find themselves in the same social position: at once superior and inferior to their partners, and therefore bound to each other by the same twofold relation that will thereafter oblige them to help each other, to share their resources and to stand with the other in disputes and conflicts between lineages and clans. The marriage alliance thus creates an enduring bond that obliges the reciprocal commitment of the members of both lineages.

We see that the marriage alliance thus adds to the strength and resources of each of the partners the strength and advantages flowing from their reciprocal debt. From this we understand that it is in the interest of each lineage to contract alliances with several other partners, who then form an ever stronger network but one that is also susceptible to cracking or dissolving in the face of disputes over land, women or cattle, for example.

You also mentioned systems in which it is the women who exchange the men.

Yes, another type of alliance, which is quite rare and even more surprising for Westerners, is the exchange of men by women. This form is found only in societies with a strongly matrilineal kinship system. It is the women who govern the matrilines, who exchange their sons, their nephews or their brothers with each other. Such is the rule among the Rhades of Vietnam, the Tetum of Timor, the Nagovisi of Bougainville, the Makhuwa of Mozambique and so on. All of these societies are matrilineal, and residence is uxorilocal or matrilocal.

Among the Tetum, the men go from their mother's house (matrilocal residence) to that of their wife (uxori-local residence). The wife's house is usually built near the big house of a female elder who governs the matri-line. It is she who keeps the cult objects and the relics of the men and women of the lineage. Each house is divided into two spaces: the women live inside, while the men live on a large platform outside; one side is occupied by the husbands, and the other, by the broth-ers, sons and nephews of the women of the house.

In this type of society, the women wield real polit-ical and ritual power, which obliges us to conclude that male domination, if it exists, takes a much softer form here. This is not to deny that men's domination of women is a nearly universal reality; but it must also be said that it is not the universal basis of kinship relations. This observation partially invalidates Lévi-Strauss's definition of kinship. For him, kinship is based on 'the exchange of women by men and for men'. Furthermore, in societies practising the exchange of women, the exchanging groups are made up not only of men, but of both men and women, who also have a say.

Of course, there are societies which do not exchange a person for a person.

Yes, in many cases, a society exchanges wealth for a woman or for a man (bride price or marriage compensation). In societies where wealth is used to obtain a spouse, we see that the richest men often accumulate the most wives, and this has become one of the symbols of social status. To come back to the modern-day Baruya, their entry into the market economy has entailed a second practice used to conclude matrimonial unions: instead of the *ginamaré*, they can collect a sum of money in order to obtain a wife from another lineage, and this acts as a marriage compensation.

In India, where wife-takers are also superior to wife-givers, there is no return gift from takers to givers; on the contrary, it is the givers who are forced to accompany the free gift of their daughter with a large dowry so that the takers will accept this woman as a wife. The reason lies in India's religious system and in the idea that a woman's body is a source of pollution once her blood flows periodically at the time of her menses. The father ensures his daughter's upkeep while she is a child but then is supposed to marry her off at puberty (and while she is still a virgin). It is up to the takers to transform, through marriage, this dangerous fertility into a source of life through procreation. Furthermore, it must not be forgotten that in India, a man or a woman must never marry someone outside their caste.

And then some systems combine unions within one's own group and unions with other groups.

Let us come back to the example of the so-called Arab marriage: according to the Koran, a Muslim may have four wives plus concubines. The first wife, as we have seen, can be the daughter of his father's brother, that is, of his paternal uncle (marriage within one's own group); but the next three possible unions are open to other choices. As a second choice a man could reproduce his father's marriage and take a woman from his mother's clan, which would strengthen the bonds between the two clans. Or he could take a woman in a clan with which his own clan has never contracted an alliance. Finally, for his fourth marriage, if he has the means, he can marry a woman from another tribe and thus establish ties between his tribe and that of his wife. Clearly, these four unions constitute a veritable matrimonial strategy, driven not by love but by other interests.

The different kinship systems also result in different forms of family. There are polygamous families (where a man marries successively or simultaneously several women): this was often the case in the Arab Muslim world or in sub-Saharan Africa. There are monogamous, nuclear families (where an individual can have only one legal partner): this is the most common case in Western societies, where polygamy is illegal in the eyes of the state. There are extended families and, more rarely, polyandrous families (where several men – usually brothers – take the same woman): this is the case in Tibet and parts of the Amazon basin (where several men who are not brothers can marry the same woman). Meanwhile today in Western societies there are more and more single-parent families, made up in the great majority of a woman and her children from different unions, which she raises alone.

Let me conclude by saying that the exchanges which seal an alliance are always fundamentally exchanges that transfer from one group to another rights over the persons who leave one group and attach themselves to the other. With the exception of the traditional Chinese culture, where the woman who left her clan ceased being a member of it once she married, most detachments and attachments are never as complete. Among the rights on persons transferred from one group to another, we can mention, in first place, the right to sexual relations when they become officially authorized. To these we must add the rights to domestic services, but also and especially rights to the women's or the men's procreative capacities and rights therefore for the affines in the children born of these unions. We must also add rights to cooperation in production when the families and lineages are themselves production and exchange units, and therefore rights to a share of the things produced by these social units. Finally, they acquire rights to mutual aid, to solidarity when it comes to political and social conflicts, and also the right to participate in rituals and other ceremonies for the ancestors, spirits or gods.

What about the dissolution of marriages?

Depending on the society, the dissolution of marriage is either allowed or forbidden. Often in societies practising the exchange of women, divorce is forbidden;

and when a woman is widowed, she is 'inherited' by her husband's brother or by one of his lineage mates (this was true until recently among the Baruya). In Tuareg society, custom has it that sons return to their father and girls to their mother. And in matrilineal societies, since a woman's children do not belong to the husband, divorce is much more prevalent than in patrilineal societies.

There is also the question of celibacy and unmarried persons in these societies.

In many societies, it is unthinkable and even forbidden to remain unmarried. It is the duty of each and every man and woman to marry and to extend the lives of their families and lineages. In the Inca Empire, all men from the age of twenty-five and all women from the age of fourteen had to be either married or promised in marriage. To this end, the imperial administration made systematic censuses of the populations and forced into marriage those who put off marrying, sometimes going as far as to impose a spouse.

And yet, celibacy is also valued in many societies when associated with the exercise of an important social function (religious, for instance) that demands that an individual renounce partially or completely sexual activities and a family – this is the case of Catholic priests and also of many Buddhist monks.

What representations of the child are associated with the different kinship systems, and what is the role of the man and the woman in the conception and birth of children? Do these representations influence the definition of incest?

To answer this question, we need to compare the representation of the way a child is made in several societies. Take the Baruya society, a patrilineal society in New Guinea. The Baruya believe that for a child to be conceived, the two sexes must unite. In this union, the sperm, called 'penis water', is deposited in the uterus, which is seen as a bag. The sperm makes the bones, flesh and blood of the child, who as a foetus has no eyes, nose, mouth, fingers or toes. For the Baruya, another actor then intervenes, which is invisible: this is the Sun, a god that gives the foetus a human form by endowing it with a mouth, fingers and so on, and with breath. Moreover, in rites addressed to the sun, the Baruya invoke it using the term *noumwé*, 'father'. At birth, the child has a human form but it is not yet a social being because it lacks a name.

Before the Europeans arrived, it was customary to hide the newborn's face from its father for its first year of life, because it had not yet received a name. If the child died during this period, its mother would bury it in uncleared ground. When the child was a year old, it received its first name, since Baruya boys and girls are initiated and receive two names over their lifetime: the name they bear before their initiation will be abandoned after this ritual and they will be given a second name, which they carry for the rest of their life. The name is always that of a male or female ancestor from the patrilineal clan to which the child belongs by birthright. The ancestral name given the child also means that the ancestor will become present in the child, but the child will not remember anything of the lives of all those who have borne the same name.

For boys, initiation is a second birth, this time at the hands of men and without the intervention of women. This second birth takes place during the male initiations, in the course of which the boy will go through several stages. During the first and second stages, and until puberty, he will be the sexual partner of the third- and fourth-stage initiates. This sexual relation consists in the elder boys having the younger boys swallow their semen, the elder boys being considered as young men pure of all pollution coming from women.

Later, for the first few weeks of a new couple's marriage, the man is supposed to have his young wife swallow his semen in the belief that it will change into the milk she will feed the baby when it is born. Semen thus signifies in part life, but also the man's strength and his superiority over women.

From this brief description of the role of men and women in making a Baruya child, we see that social representations give the man's role much more importance than that of the woman who carries the child and gives birth to it. But we also see that a man and a woman are not sufficient to make this child, since two other, invisible actors intervene: the sun, in the role of deity, and the ancestor, who gives his or her name to the child after its birth.

I would add that the Baruya's definition of incest is based on the fact that their kinship system is of what anthropologists call the 'Iroquois' type: all of the mother's sisters are mothers, and all of the father's brothers are fathers. The incest taboo thus covers more than simply the nuclear family; it applies to these different fathers and mothers, as well as to their descendants.

A contrasting example is that of the Trobriand Islanders, a matrilineal-descent society. In this society, sexual intercourse does not result in the conception of a child. Young people have sexual relations before marriage, but these relations are meant to open the young women to penetration by a male or female ancestor spirit who wishes to become re-embodied in one of their descendants. In this society, it is believed that the deceased live under the rule of the god of the dead in a nearby island, and that from time to time, one of them desires to be reborn. So it takes the form of a spirit-child and leaves the island to enter the body of a young woman, where it mixes with her menstrual blood, thus making a foetus. In this representation, the man's sperm is in no way at the origin of the conception of a child. The woman alone engenders the child, with the help of her ancestors. What does the sperm do? It is used to nourish the foetus and, for this reason, as soon as a woman realizes she is pregnant, the couple increase their sexual relations to nourish the foetus, but also, it seems, to mould its outer shape. The result is that, in this society where children do not belong to the father, it is still said that they all look like the man who is the mother's husband. The father is thus a social, and not a biological, father, since his sperm does not engender the child that will be born. And, as I have said, in this society, father/daughter incest is not recognized.

A third example of a patrilineal society which recognizes the role of women in making a child is that of the Khumbo farmer-herders living in the so-called 'hidden' valley of Arun, in Nepal. This is an interesting case because the people are the descendants of refugees who left the initial Tibetan kingdoms before they converted to Buddhism. This society continues to celebrate pre-Buddhist rites even though it recently converted to Buddhism.

Their adherence to two religions also finds expression in the way the society represents the conception of a child. For the Khumbo, sexual relations are required to make a child: the man's sperm is believed to make the embryo's bones and brain, while the woman adds her blood and her flesh. The society is patrilineal, and the bones made by the man's sperm are considered to create a bond between individuals and their clan deity.

In the end, the child receives two souls. The first is a life principle (*la*) which connects it to the mountain gods, masters of the territory. This principle stems from Tibetan pre-Buddhist religious representations. A second soul (*namsche*) is the vehicle for the (illusory) perception individuals have of the world and of themselves. It is the vehicle of the actions that will keep individuals imprisoned in the cycle of reincarnations or, on the contrary, will liberate them. It is therefore clear that, in this society, once again, a man and a woman do not suffice to make a child; other actors must intervene, among whom are mountain gods and the representations of life and death found in Buddhism.

The last society is that of the Na, a Tibeto-Burman group of agriculturalists, herders and merchants living in the Chinese province of Yunnan. The Na are the most strongly matrilineal society known: it has large matri-lines composed of the descendants of the female founder of the line. The matriline is made up of women and their brothers, as well as the children born to these women. Women have responsibility for and authority over housework and worship. Trade and exchanges with other societies fall to their brothers.

The particularity of this society is that it does not recognize the institution of marriage; its language does not have a word for husband or father. In this case, the representations of father/daughter incest do not have the same meaning. If there is no marriage in this soci-ety, it is because men and women customarily come together during night-time encounters that take place as follows: at night, the women's brothers leave their sisters and go to spend the night with women of other matrilines, while the men from other matrilines come to visit the others' sisters. The choice of a sexual part-ner is always up to the woman. A woman can thus sleep with one man one week, and with his brother the next. If deeper feelings develop, the woman must ask the members of her line as a whole permission to receive the man not only at night but in the daytime as well.

How does this society represent the conception of a child?

The man's sperm is not at the origin of the birth of a child. Here, too, semen is regarded as 'penis water', which causes the embryos deposited by a goddess in the belly of baby girls to grow. The semen waters these foetuses and nourishes them, but it does not engender them. The woman is considered to make, with the help of the goddess, the child's bones and flesh. Just the opposite of the patrilineal Khumbo, the matriline here is called 'the people of one bone'. This is a society in which there is no exchange of persons between kin groups; instead, exchanges of sperm lead to exchanges without alliance or marriage, since there is no such thing as marriage and therefore no vocabulary for affines. The mutual aid between the sexes thus takes place between brothers and sisters, uncles and aunts, nephews and nieces, and so forth. However, the incest taboo is altogether present, even to the point of strictly forbidding any mention of sexuality within the matriline. In the event of mother/son incest or uncle or aunt with nephew or niece, the guilty party is put to death.

Does the definition and prohibition of incest apply equally to all members of society?

No. Representations of kinship relations and taboos can vary within a society from one group to the next, depending on the groups that form the social hierarchy. For instance, in Bali, when opposite-sex twins are born in an aristocratic family, the birth is considered divine, and the twins are welcomed as already united by the gods; at adolescence the twin couple is married. On the other hand, if opposite-sex twins are born to a commoner, they are considered as bearers of incest; the parents are banished, and the village where the children were born must be ritually purified. So we see that the same reality is declared incestuous or not depending on the social status of the partners.

To sum up: in very rare cases, we find brother–sister marriages, whose status is, as we have seen, exceptional. These unions constitute intrafamilial alliances without exchange. However, most kinship systems are based on alliances with exchange (of usually women but sometimes men) between kin groups. Finally, the example of the Na is altogether exceptional because there we have exchanges of sperm between kin groups without the groups ever contracting matrimonial alliances with each other. This is why this system not only has no words for father and husband, it has none for father-in-law or mother-in-law either. Which introduces the sixth and last component of all kinship systems: the existence in the language of a specific vocabulary for the kinship positions and relations.

But it seems to me you have forgotten adoption among the forms of kinship.

Indeed. Adoption is a perfect example of the social aspect of kinship, since it creates descendants without conception. The child's birth ascendants are replaced by its adoptive kin. In Ancient Rome, only a man possessed of the *patria potestas* could adopt another human, provided that their age difference corresponded roughly to that between two generations. But adoption is not a general phenomenon. For example, during the Western European Middle Ages, the Catholic Church not only banned divorce and blocked the remarriage of widows, but also forbade adoption while promoting the celibacy of priests. For this reason, adoption reappeared in the different European legal systems only at the end of the nineteenth century.

Today France recognizes two types of adoption: full adoption and simple adoption. Full adoption is a legal fiction which purely and simply erases the adoptees' relation to their birth family and replaces it with a pseudo-genealogical position in the adopting family: the adopters have the same rights and same duties as the child's birth parents. In the case of simple adoption, on the other hand, children keep their original identity. In both types of adoption, sexual relations between parents and children are prohibited. In theory, Islam forbids adoption because the Prophet repudiates it in the Koran.

Coming back to the sixth component of all kinship systems: how do languages express kinship relations and positions between individuals and social groups?

All languages have a specific vocabulary for kinship relations – father, mother and so on – and for the acts that produce these relations (such as marriage) or, on the contrary, that produce the dissolution of a union (divorce or separation). The first type of vocabulary is made up of a set of reference terms to designate the fact of kinship (such as being the father, or father-in-law), marriage, divorce, an incestuous relation and so on. The other vocabulary is composed of terms of address used in private with close kin (for example, daddy, mummy, grandpa, grandma).

Kinship terminologies manifest, in their structure, the nature of the kinship system for which they are the linguistic vehicle. Our inventory of kinship systems has allowed us to distinguish seven types spread over the face of the globe. These are the systems known as Dravidian, Australian, Iroquois, Crow-Omaha, Sudanese, Hawaiian and the so-called 'Eskimo' system, which is found not only among the Inuit but also in Western Europe and in South-East Asia.

Note that in the Western system, certain terms form categories, since the term 'uncle' designates both the father's brother and the mother's brother as well as the father's sister's husband or the mother's sister's husband, and likewise for the terms for cousins. If we compare this system (Eskimo), where the individual has only one father, with the Baruya system (Iroquois), where the individual has several fathers and several mothers, we observe that the notions of father, mother and sibling (brothers and sisters) are completely different and cannot be thought and experienced in the same way. Which also explains the position and the different nature of the incest taboo.

Chapter 3

The Sexed Body of Men and Women: Ventriloquist's Dummies for Their Society

How then are we to interpret these different representations of men's and women's sexed bodies, their bodily secretions (sperm, menstrual blood, mother's milk and so on), which seem purely imaginary representations for us today?

To be sure, we can think that no one has ever seen 'sperm' change into mother's milk or menstrual blood transform into the flesh and blood of an embryo. It is likely that no one has ever seen an ancestor spirit or the Holy Spirit take possession of the child's body forming in its mother's womb and animate it by endowing it with a soul and a spirit. However, for a long time, no one had ever seen a sperm fertilize an egg either, and only a few persons have witnessed it today ... All of these representations are produced by the mind seeking to understand and explain how life is reproduced while at the same time legitimizing a social order inscribed in the body, an order that is, at the same time, the relationship between the sexes: in other words, a sexual order.

These representations may be imaginary for us, but for those who believe in them, they are obvious truths. Let us go back, for example, to the significations attaching to sperm among the Baruya of New Guinea, as featured in their patrilineal kinship system. Sperm is the first agent activated in making a child, and that justifies the child belonging from birth to its father's clan and not to its mother's.

For Trobriand Islanders, on the other hand, it is the menstrual blood that helps make the child's body, and this receives an ancestor spirit which wants to begin a new life. This, in turn, legitimizes the child belonging from birth to its mother's clan and not to its father's. In both cases, body substances (sperm and menstrual blood) are overvalued, while others are minimized or downgraded (deemed dangerous).

In these two societies, no one thinks that sexual intercourse between a man and a woman is *sufficient* to make a child. The mind is, therefore, obliged to imagine that other, invisible, actors intervene in this process. The child thus finds itself inscribed from the outset in a totality that is at once cosmic and social, and which will be its life-long environment.

But such representations of the sexed body of men and women do more than simply legitimize the child's membership of a given group of adults who are its relatives; they also serve to legitimize the unequal power relations prevailing between men and women, and also between the kin groups to which the child belongs.

Let us come back to the role and signification of sperm in Baruya society. Not only is this substance supposed to make a child's embryo, but, at the same time, it enables men to be reborn a second time, this time without the intervention of women. This rebirth is carried out in the course of male initiations, in which young boys who have never had sexual relations with a woman regularly 'inseminate' younger boys who have been separated from their mother and the female world for years. The Baruya's ritual homosexuality, in a way, transmutes the male body with respect to that of women. One proof of this is that as soon as a boy is initiated, he becomes the elder of all his brothers and sisters, whatever their chronological age. That is why the Baruya consider menstrual blood to be a constant threat to their strength and to their superiority with respect to women.

This clearly shows that the body, as a set of visible and invisible components, is, in every society, recruited – with the aid of ideological explanations that obey a set code of symbols – to serve both the production and the reproduction not only of relations between kin groups, but also of the political-religious relations that encompass them. These political-religious relations together with kinship relations are the sites of the social power that prevails in a society.

In other words, the stakes and consequences of these imaginary representations and their symbolic force are thus neither imaginary nor purely symbolic?

That's right. They serve to legitimize men's power and their domination over women as much as the domination of one class or one caste over the others in society.

Under the Ancien Régime in France, society was dominated by the nobility, whose members claimed to have 'blue blood', unlike the blood flowing in commoners' veins; and that justified their position and power in society, their supremacy over commoners.

There is, thus, a twofold social process at work in all societies: social and material realities having *nothing to do* with kinship or sexuality – for example, private ownership of the land, access to ritual or political functions – infiltrate kinship relations and press them into their service, into the service of their own reproduction. It will be the eldest son who inherits land, not a younger one; among the Tetum, it will be the eldest female member of the matriline who inherits religious functions, and so on. In short, economic relations and social functions metamorphose into attributes of certain kinship relations which, ultimately, become attributes of the persons who occupy this place in the relations.

What do you mean by 'metamorphose'?

I mean that social attributes become kinship attributes, which, in turn, become sexual attributes, attributes of persons according to sex, age and place in the family, the lineage, the clan and so on. Through this twofold metamorphosis, found in all societies, social realities having nothing to do with kinship infiltrate the kinship structure and make it the prime site of the individual's socialization, of their appropriation by the society.

All of the above remarks converge towards a fundamental fact: in all societies, the sexed body of an individual works like a ventriloquist's dummy for society. Sexed, socialized bodies are transformed into *genders* – male and female. But this subordination of kinship and sexuality to the reproduction of areas of life that have nothing to do with sexuality is a subordination not only of the relations between persons: this subordination manifests the importance that the society gives to other domains of social life – relations with the gods, political power, wealth, economic strength and so on.

In the case of humans, the sexed body is the site of a two-sided sexuality: sexuality-as-desire, and the sexuality-for-reproduction that is implemented in the production of kinship relations and in the reproduction of human groups. These two kinds of sexuality are distinct and disconnected: the desire and pleasure connected with the sex act are distinct from the desire to reproduce. Sexual desire is sparked as much by internal representations as by external stimulation. In all societies, desire can be satisfied by relations that are heterosexual, homosexual and autosexual (masturbation). Human sexuality is spontaneous, unconstrained by seasons and aroused by representations (cerebration), polymorphous (homo- and heterosexual), polytropic (can direct itself to any other), and can be disjoined from the reproduction of life. Each society ascribes different but interdependent significations to these forms of sexuality. But the world over, sexuality-as-desire can be opposed to socialized, domesticated sexuality, which has become the society's ventriloquist dummy, has become *gender*.

For you, then, there is nothing negative about the notion of 'gender', which has been the object of much political and ideological debate in the past few years.

As I have defined it, 'gender' is not an ideological notion. It is indispensable in showing the possibilities and impossibilities societies attribute to persons according to their sex. This is a recent and fundamental finding in the social sciences.

This socialization, this domestication, occurs during infancy and adolescence. These are the two decisive life stages when a child learns to behave correctly. They are the times when, as soon as sexual desire appears, it is channelled by adult family members and their social group towards the 'appropriate' persons, those authorized by the society. In most cases, this bending of desire to conform to the social and sexual order supposed to reign in the society occurs silently: it is unspoken and will go on to work in the individual's subconscious. In this way, individuals are expected, through the way they use their body, to attest both to the order reigning in society and perhaps even to the order that should continue to reign.

Therefore, in any society, sexuality must adopt forms that are self-evident to one and all. Sexual and affective desires are socialized and brought into agreement so that they will not threaten the social order. In the end, society subsists through but also beyond the realization of individual desires. It is not surprising, then, that those who reject the surrounding social and sexual order also manifest this with their bodies – some undergo scarification, some dye their hair, others paint their body, and so on.

Finally, what does the incest taboo inscribe in the individual?

What the incest taboo inscribes in the individual is not only the idea that the uses of sex should be subservient to the reproduction of society. It is also, and on a much deeper level, that sexuality should be placed in the service of this reproduction. But for this to come about, something of the spontaneous polyvalence of desire – hetero- and homosexual – must be amputated. It is this irreducible law that is imprinted by the many forms of incest and sexual taboos. But this partial amputation of desire, its domestication, does not destroy the individual; it works to promote a specifically human trait, namely humans' generic capacity not only to live in society but to produce society in order to live.

Can we say that for those who initiate an incestuous sexual relation, the transgression of this taboo is a source simultaneously of pleasure and fear? And what about for the victim of force and violence or persuasion and seduction?

I think that those who commit such acts do so consciously, to satisfy their desires. They are therefore seeking pleasure – and domination. At the same time, they are aware that it is forbidden – and there is pleasure in transgression – and they also feel fear (fear of discovery and punishment). For the victims, whether they have been forced or seduced, the damage to their personal equilibrium, the loss of references, is extremely serious and usually lasts for life if there is no means to bring the situation to light and talk about it so that the perpetrator of the inner violence is punished.

Often, in police investigations of incest, the affair is discovered by the school, which sees a child who is disturbed and clearly suffering before discovering the reality once trust has been established. Does this discovery, when it is reported to the police, always lead to an investigation, to social repression? I don't know. But I repeat: incest destroys the responsibility, authority and protection that family members owe each other in order to sustain their social ties and maintain a social and personal equilibrium.

What trove of information do anthropologists have on cases of incest in Western countries?

We have a considerable amount of data on father/ daughter incest and that between stepfather and step-daughter, probably the most frequent case and in which a relation of male domination plays a large role. We have very little information on mother/son incest and even less on cases of homosexual incest. The last two forms of incest are rarely reported to the police by neighbours. We would certainly need to know more about the reasons that drive a mother to seduce her son. It is likely that the relations of affection and even a symbiotic relationship between mother and son may be the preconditions, but this does not explain the mother's desire to have sexual relations with her son and to form a couple. While the existence of an element of male domination in father/daughter relations is recognized, it is likely that there is an element of female domination in the mother/son relationship. But the mother/son relation probably is more affective and fusional than the father/daughter relationship.

Do anthropologists have data on the consequences of breaking the incest taboo in other societies?

We do. And the consequences take two forms: social punishment and divine punishment. The Baruya told me that if they surprised a brother and sister making love, they killed them: they disembowelled them and hung their intestines on their garden fence. But that was more a statement of a social norm than a reference to actual cases of incest committed in the past. In Bali, for example, in the event of brother/sister incest among the poor, their villages could be burned, and the population exiled. In many societies, divine punishments are mentioned – drought, famine and so on. Often, incest is considered to be a stain on the group as a whole and requires that the whole population undergo rites of purification.

Chapter 4
From Animal to Human

Do you think, like Lévi-Strauss, that the prohibition of incest allowed humans to emerge from their animal state?

Nature gave our male or female bodies their anatomic and physiological sexual traits, which enable our social species to reproduce; but sexual desire itself can turn spontaneously towards persons that are socially forbidden. It is by no means impossible that a son may desire his mother – which, in itself, is proof that it must be forbidden. In this sense, human sexuality is fundamentally *a-social*. For over 120,000 years, *Homo sapiens sapiens* has been experimenting with very different ways of organizing society and has reached the universal conclusion that it is necessary to curb sexual permissiveness. Because sexuality is also a source of conflicts, it cannot be entirely left up to each individual.

Another way of approaching the question would be to ask if we find the equivalent of the incest taboo in other animal species.

We can answer this question only by comparing humans with the two primate species closest to us, with which we share over 90 per cent of our chromosomes: chimpanzees and bonobos. Humans are, in fact, one of the 152 primate species living on the planet today. Of course, when making this comparison, we must avoid projecting specifically human lifestyles onto bonobos or chimpanzees; we must not anthropomorphize them.

It should be remembered that chimpanzees, bonobos and humans all descend from a common ancestor; and the ancestor of all of the hominid species that have since appeared split off from the chimpanzee and bonobo lines six million years ago. Then, we are told, chimpanzees and bonobos themselves separated two million years later. Today, of the fifty-two behaviours observed in the two species, only twenty-five are common to both.

Both bonobos and chimpanzees live in bands containing multiple males and females that exploit the material resources of a territory, which the band members strive to control and to defend against the intrusion of neighbouring bands. The existence of

bands is thus the indispensable condition for the existence and survival of their individual members. As the
biologist François Jacob wrote in *The Logic of Life*
(first published in French in 1970), for certain species,
including our own, society is the necessary environment
for an individual of these species to develop to its
fullest. For Jacob, the notion of 'environment' included
not only exploitable resources but also the social organization of the individuals.

So, for chimpanzees and bonobos, society exists, but
it does not have families that unite in a stable fashion
a male and one or several females and their offspring.
Females live on their own with their young at the centre
of the territory, and they are the ones who feed and
raise them. Chimpanzees communicate with others
using a certain number of vocalizations, each of which
has a different meaning: the arrival of a predator,
discovery of a fruiting tree, and so on. To these vocalizations are added gestures, body postures, behaviours
(such as grooming), which have meaning for all
members of the band. Chimpanzees make, carry and
use tools, but they do not make tools for making tools.
They engage in collective hunting and attack small
antelope, as well as other primate species. They kill
and share out the bodies of their victims on the spot
and have been seen to wage veritable wars with other

bands, in the course of which the adults of one band (males but also females) enter the territory of another band and kill one or more of its members.

The social organization of a chimpanzee band is based on the combination of forms of cooperation, as in hunting, and forms of competition: between males, between males and females, and between females. This results in the formation of a hierarchy within the band according to age and sex, a hierarchy that, though not fixed, can sometimes persist for years. Observers were struck by the important discovery that conflicts between individuals within a band are limited, for these conflicts never drive the loser out. The winner holds out an upturned hand to the loser, who touches it; this gesture is followed by hugging, stroking, mutual grooming and sexual relations. It is as though, by setting a limit on their conflicts, the members of a band act in a way such that the band can continue to exist.

Sexual relations among chimpanzees take three forms, which anthropologists have called opportunistic, possessive and couple formation. The opportunistic type corresponds to the period when the females are in season, during which time a female is approached and mounted successively by a number of males; the possessive type can be seen during the same period, when a dominant male takes possession of a receptive female and keeps other males away by charging them.

The third type was also an important discovery: it was observed that a male and a female with young sometimes distance themselves from the rest of the band for hours and sometimes days; their preferential liaison comes to an end whenever the female wants, and responds to the calls of the other males, whom she directs towards herself. Outside mating season, chimpanzees and bonobos express their sexuality in other forms – homosexual and autosexual. But in neither species is there any sign that males recognize their genetic offspring among the young.

Is the same true of bonobos?

Bonobo social organization is more centred on the females, and the males are relatively hostile to each other and do not form alliances. They do not engage in collective hunting or share kill between males and females. A high-ranking female may even impose herself in front of the alpha male. Mothers have a strong attachment to their sons and defend them if need be. Both bonobos and chimpanzees mature slowly and relatively late – at between eight and ten years of age – while for humans, this is between twelve and fourteen.

Bonobos are distinctive in that they sometimes mate face to face, like humans.

In both species, individual sexuality serves, as among humans, to produce social relations; it is important to note that there, too, the individual's sexuality is subordinated to the production of their social way of life. But, unlike humans, primates do not have the capacity to change the rules governing their social life.

Do we find biological mechanisms in these primate societies that would prevent genetically close individuals from having sexual relations and would protect their descendants against genetic disasters resulting from uniting with a closely related mate? In other words, is there avoidance of incest among primates?

Observers have noted that, after a longer or shorter period of attachment to their young, females undertake a process of detachment, but they do not treat sons and daughters the same way; they are more aggressive with their sons. The young male then gradually turns to the other females in his band. But above all, when the young females reach puberty, they leave the band, one by one, and join neighbouring bands, where the fact of being outsiders makes them more attractive to the local males. There are two opposing forces, then, that influence these primates' sexuality: forces that repel and forces that attract, which orient individual sexuality and relations.

When these observations were published, certain ethologists immediately began talking about exogamy and exchange of females between bands, and even about matrilineal bands among the bonobos, and so on. Actually, it seems that the purpose of these opposing forces is not to limit consanguineous mating in order to avoid negative genetic consequences, but to regulate individuals' sexual development from infancy to the end of adolescence so that the pursuit of their new-found sexual desire does not endanger the reproduction of the local band in which they grew up.

In effect, it has been observed that when the young males' sexuality begins to manifest, it remains inhibited for months by the power relations and hierarchy between the males of the band. Their access to receptive females or to the young females arriving from other bands is blocked by the adult males. For as long as the young males have not made a place for themselves in the male hierarchy, they will be denied access to receptive females.

This double mechanism whereby the young pubescent females leave the bands and outside females arrive seems therefore not to be a matter of incest avoidance but a way of regulating the social and sexual life of the members of each band by eliminating the possibility of conflicts between adult and juvenile males. At the same time, because the now-receptive young females have left, the adult males can no longer mate with those whom they could not recognize as their daughters; likewise, for the young males, who, in turn, could not know who were their sisters. These departures and arrivals of receptive young females thus in fact result in a genetic renewal of the bands, which is the consequence, but not the goal, of these biological mechanisms.

What these phenomena have in common with human behaviour is that biological mechanisms serve a *social regulation* of sexuality. But these mechanisms are *unconscious* among the other primates, whereas the social regulation of sexuality among humans is a conscious phenomenon.

How did the transition from the animal to the human state come about? What room is made for the incest taboo? Were there several points of passage?

Indeed. Humans are a naturally social species: in other words, we can survive only in society. The difference with the other social animals is that humans, thanks to their cognitive capacities, to the development of their brain, are permanently obliged and able to invent new forms of society in order to live. Our species, *Homo sapiens sapiens*, emerged 120,000 years ago or more; it has thus had time to experiment with many forms of social organization, and to conclude, gradually and universally, that sexual permissiveness needed to be curbed: that sexuality needed to be domesticated in each of us, because it needed constantly to be subordinated to the reproduction of social relations – which it invented (in the form of political, religious and economic relations, for example, that concern all of the social groups within a given society). It must be stressed that between our animal ancestor and all of the varieties of hominins that have existed, down to the emergence of our species, hundreds of thousands of years have elapsed, creating a growing distance between these hominins and their animal ancestor.

There was thus not only one condition for the passage from the animal to the human state; there were several others, which even preceded the appearance of our own species. Today, we know that several hominin species descending from a common ancestor appeared and coexisted until the time the Neanderthals disappeared, leaving only our species. It seems that as early as *Homo habilis* (500,000 BCE), those remote ancestors had already domesticated fire. The domestication of fire opened up a huge new domain of food resources and created social relationships for sharing and consuming this food – raw and cooked. With cooking came the domestic hearth, which appeared as the site and crucible of new relations between men and women, and between adults and children; and these relations were at once social, material and affective.

Another point of passage was the sexual division of tasks. We saw that among the higher apes, the females raise and feed their children by themselves. This was probably not the case for early hominins and is not at all the case for our species. We also know that the Neanderthals buried their dead, sometimes adding man-made objects to accompany them into the other world. This means that this species, which lived in parallel with our own, already had a metaphysical view of life and death, and manipulated symbols.

Yet another point of transition was the capacity for articulated language, which enabled us to create the many languages we speak and whose words are the symbolic vehicles of thought. *Homo sapiens'* brain probably developed in connection with the complexity of the tasks our ancestors learned to perform (such as making tools with which to make other tools), with the complexity of the social relations they entertained and with the complexity of the problems they had to resolve in order to survive. Hence human thought allowed humankind to analyse the past and to imagine possible futures. It is in this context that we can understand the other transition point, which was the invention of the incest taboo.

These different moments and forms of distancing and transformation in hominins with respect to their original animal state were ultimately implemented and synthesized in our own species, *Homo sapiens sapiens*. Lévi-Strauss had rightly identified most of these transition points – the raw and the cooked, the sexual division of tasks, articulated speech and the performances of the brain and thought, and of course the prohibition of incest. But he saw these as the consequences of a 'big bang', which he believed to be the sudden emergence of symbolic thought. It would seem that these transformations were instead both continuous and discontinuous on the path from the original animal state of hominids to the human state of *Homo sapiens sapiens*.

And so, the evolutionary history of humankind has thus become simply history – the story of the societies that have unfolded down to our day?

Yes. Over the course of this modern history, of which we catch the first glimmer very early in the Neolithic era, around 12,000 BCE, in the mountains of Turkey and on the plains of Mesopotamia, the child probably came to be an increasingly important stake for the adults owing to the new forms of power and economy emerging at that time. This was the era when plants and animals were first domesticated, which would deeply transform the economy and organization of the human groups that would gradually settle down on the land. A new distance would impose itself between primates and humans, for primates find their means of survival in nature but they do not produce these means.

The innovations comprising the development of agriculture, combined with herding in the Near East and then in Europe and Asia – of horticulture in Oceania, of nomadic herding in Central Asia and East Africa – had three consequences. First, the cooperation and material and social interdependence between men and women within new forms of division of tasks grew more complex. Second, some of the new conditions of social existence, such as growing lands, pastureland, water courses for irrigation, and so on, became fundamental stakes in the reproduction of these new forms of society. Under these conditions, the child – both as a possible source of labour but especially as a vehicle, depending on the sex (boy or girl) and the descent principle (patri-, matri- and so on) at work in the society – became the vehicle for the transmission of land ownership, wealth, status and the knowledge of the groups in which he or she had been born or adopted. More than ever, society came to have a stake in the child. The third consequence was that, with the development of certain Neolithic economies, cities appeared, leading to the separation between town and surrounding countryside. The first states arose in cities – they were the site of temples, palaces, military fortresses, the residence of the governing groups, priests, warriors, all manner of craftsmen – and so these societies became increasingly unequal, became state-run societies with ranked orders, castes or classes.

These transformations and their consequences, which can still be felt today, mean that, for the society and the adults who govern it, the child has constantly been a stake in a social strategy that no longer has anything in common with the time when humans still made their living by hunting and gathering. And yet, whatever the era, whatever the kinship system adopted by a society, however equal or unequal this society, children are all and always the fruit of a woman's womb.

**So you're saying that it became a strategic social neces-
sity to establish the social conditions in which a man
and a woman could sexually unite, and to establish at
the same time what kin group the children of these
unions would belong to?**

That's right, and, given that the birth of children always
depends on women, the control of these women by
groups and by those who held power (usually men)
became a strategic necessity for the reproduction of
the societies, for transmission and for the continuity
of the groups forming the societies. And that is the
underlying and undying source of men's domination
not only over women but also over children.

In these contexts, the moving force behind the unions
and therefore the workings of the kinship systems
invented to codify them were not, were never – until
the end of the nineteenth century – the love or sexual
desire of the men and women whom their kin group
obliged to marry. At last, the break between humans
and animals was consummated. In primate bands, there
are neither groups specialized in different tasks nor a
hierarchy designed to carry out these tasks. Whereas
in human groups, from the Neolithic era at least, there
are multiple social groups, which are all different but
necessary for the constitution of distinct societies.

Do you think that the invariables anthropologists have discovered from data gathered in numerous societies (in the East, the West or in the Americas) – about how children are made, about death, the role of humans and the gods, and so on – were formulated by humankind from the outset?

For the very beginnings of history, as long as no society had invented writing and the state, all we have are myths about the origin of fire, the origin of humans, of the sun and so on, which have come down to us today thanks to human memory and rites. But from the time the first city-states appeared in Mesopotamia, at the end of the fourth millennium BCE, and a bit later in Egypt under the pharaohs, we have many texts concerning gods, death and the afterlife, as well as treatises on medicine, divination and so on.

Reading these texts, we discover that these societies all shared several conclusions concerning human existence. First of all, the fact that humankind did not create itself and did not create the surrounding universe, which supposed that other, more powerful actors, created them. This conclusion is the starting point for all religions. These societies also concluded that death was not the opposite of life but the opposite of birth. They assumed that the deceased went to an abode of the dead where they continued another form of existence – we have only to think of the practice of mummification in Ancient Egypt.

But they still had to understand how a human being was born, and it seems that, very early on, humans deemed that a man and a woman did not suffice to make a child but that other actors intervened to make and animate it. Finally, reading the legal texts, it seems that humans had already discovered that it was important for the groups that composed the society both to know how to give in order to contract alliances and to keep what needed to be transmitted in order to continue to exist.

The religious treatises and ancient codes of law would be incomprehensible if human thinking had not already reached these four conclusions. And, once these conclusions were reached, they became the principles presiding over the organization of societies, over the creation of their religious and political institutions. But these conclusions were not restricted to state-based societies, since anthropologists have also found them in tribal societies (egalitarian or not) and they were preserved until these societies were discovered by the West in its global colonial expansion.

We must therefore conclude that as humankind evolved and entered the course of history, it became the only species to exercise co-responsibility with nature for its own evolution. And that is because we are the only species capable of acting on ourselves by inventing other ways of living while acting on nature to procure our means of existence.

But are there conditions found at all times and in all societies that must be met in order for a new human being to come into the world?

Indeed. A child is born with a body and a sex it has not chosen, and which it owes to the human, and some-times non-human, actors that made it. It can survive and grow only if it is cared for by adults, who usually do this because of the kinship relations that bind them to the child. Furthermore, a child is always born into a society and at a time it has not chosen. It is born in a society where the language that is spoken and which it will learn as well carries the basic components of this society's culture and organization. And the child has not chosen its language either. Finally, a child is born, survives and grows up in a social group it has not chosen, and which always occupies a defined place in the society. Its life path will then be determined by the place and moment of its birth. In India, the son of Brahmins will be a Brahmin; in a Muslim country, a boy or girl will be Muslim by birth; and in a Christian country, the children will become Christians through baptism, and so on.

These five prior conditions which define and accompany a child's birth are universal, and mean that, everywhere, a child is, at birth, a biological, social and historical being. From the outset the child always grows up and is socialized within a given society and culture, at a certain point in time. Culture is not something that is added to biology; it permeates it from birth.

It should be noted that these components are not a matter of individual choice; they are givens which always determine the starting point from which a human is going to construct or undergo their life.

Chapter 5
The Child and Kinship Today

What about kinship relations and the children born in Western societies today, which claim to be founded on individual freedom and aspire to promote the fulfilment of this freedom?

This is a big question. In response, I will content myself with some references to recent developments in France. Four things have changed in the West since the Second World War: our relation to sexuality; the place of children in society; relations between men and women and the struggle to make them less unequal; and the evolution of the forms of parenthood thanks to the emergence of new technologies and the acquisition of new freedoms.

When it comes to our relation to sexuality, we have seen that young people are allowed to have sexual relations at an ever earlier age, even if the average age at which they become sexually active seems to have stabilized. Furthermore, we have observed that adolescents are increasingly influenced by pornographic films, which influence their representations of sexuality and no doubt their future sexual relations.

The sexual liberation was facilitated by the appearance of contraceptives. Among these, 'the pill', approved in the US in 1960 and authorized in France in 1970, enabled women to take control of their bodies and have children if and when they wished and not when they were obliged to. To this possibility of liberation, France in 1975 added the decriminalization of abortion under certain conditions. The outcome of these gains was that the birth of a child became increasingly the birth of a child that was wanted, and not a child that was imposed.

In the West, from Jean-Jacques Rousseau's *Emile* (1762) and down to the United Nations Convention on the Rights of the Child (adopted in 1989), the child and childhood have become a dominant preoccupation. Recognition of the rights of children – their protection from abuse that adults, including parents, might inflict, recognition of children's right to think their own thoughts – increasingly pervade Western societies. To kill children after having sexually abused them is considered by many contemporary societies as the most depraved crime.

France took a major step when paternal authority, which derives from the ancient Roman *patria potestas*, was replaced by parental authority shared equally by the two parents. This law has been enriched several times since (in 1987 and then in 1993), so that all children, whatever their parents' or guardians' legal status, might be treated equally in society. Furthermore, this law declares that the parents are morally and legally required to fulfil their parental responsibilities until the child's majority in four domains essential to their development: safety; education; health; and appropriate guidance and direction. These responsibilities are incumbent on parents whatever their chosen lifestyle and, in view of ensuring the continuity of the parents' responsibility, independently of separation, divorce or other disruptions to the parental couple.

Isn't it increasingly the case, in our Western societies, that both men and women express the desire to have a child, even absent marriage or other forms of union, through adoption or insemination in the case of single women?

Yes. In the West, scientific progress has opened up new ways of having children. We have seen the birth of children stemming from two men and a woman, or two women and a man. In the first event, a couple in which the man turns out to be sterile accepts and decides that another man's sperm will be used to fertilize his partner's egg. The child is then genetically and socially related to its mother but not to the man, who becomes its social father. In this case, it has been found that a man does not feel less of a man because he knows himself to be sterile. What matters to him is to have a child with his partner, whom they will raise together.

This is not the first time (and not only in the West) that society has invented exceptional solutions to deal with difficult problems. For instance, among the Nuer, an ethnic group living in Sudan, if a man dies leaving his widow childless, the woman has the choice of marrying another woman. In reality, by paying the marriage compensation a man must pay in order to marry, the widow becomes the (fictive) 'husband' of a woman and chooses a lover for her who will give her children. The children are then attributed to the deceased husband's lineage and so ensure his family's continuity.

In the case of surrogate mothers, we see an even deeper transformation of parenthood. Modern technologies in effect make it possible to separate the processes of conception and gestation. This has opened the way for couples wanting a child (but where the female partner cannot carry out a normal pregnancy) to choose this path over adoption. In adoption, I repeat, the child is an outsider who becomes, legally and fictively, a member of the family, a relative. However, when a couple turns to a surrogate mother, their child is genetically related to them, since the woman's egg, fertilized by her partner, is implanted into the surrogate mother's womb. When the child is born, it is socially and genetically fully related to its (this time both biological and social) parents.

This raises the question of whether the woman who carries out the pregnancy for another woman, with all the risks entailed in childbirth, is also a mother for the child.

In the West – the United States, Spain, Greece, the Netherlands and so on, where surrogate motherhood is legal – relations between this woman and the child's parents are defined contractually. The woman who lends her body has no rights over the child once it is born, and she receives a compensation for the loan of her body and the risks entailed in childbirth. This monetary compensation is usually limited so that it is not assimilated to the purchase of a body by a couple unable to have children. It is very hard to draw the line between lending one's body in order to give a couple a child, a life, and using one's body to make money while staying at home. But a couple's desire for a child can always drive them to break the law, which is hard to enforce. In France, for instance, the state persists in denying women the possibility of carrying a child for another.

The problem remains of whether a woman who carries a child for another takes on part of the responsibilities normally incumbent on a woman when she brings a child into the world. While we may think that giving his sperm does not make a man a father and giving an egg for fertilization does not make a woman a mother, the question becomes more complicated when a woman lends her body to carry someone else's child.

All three cases, though, raise the question of whether or not to reveal to a child born in these conditions that it was the result of the gift of another's sperm, another's egg or was carried by another woman who gave birth. Is it necessary to reveal the conditions of its birth to a child who has been raised and cherished by its parents for years? Is it necessary to tell it the genealogical truth of its existence? All these problems are under debate in the West and oblige us to reconsider the definitions of fatherhood and motherhood – in sum, the two pillars of kinship.

Hasn't there been another major change in Western countries, in that, for the first time, new forms of family have been made legal after numerous battles and a great deal of resistance on the part of society: same-sex unions are now recognized?

A minority of homosexual men or women have long been demanding the right to live officially as couples and to be able, if they so desire, to found a family by adopting children or giving birth. Finally, after years of struggle, France legalized same-sex marriage in 2013. Some of the problems raised by these unions have already been resolved in court (such as the family name given a child born to a lesbian couple: the child will carry the two names); yet that may continue to cause problems for a public opinion used to the child receiving the name of a father and a mother.

In the case of homosexual unions, too, the problem of secrecy about the child's origins comes up. For it is always with the help of a sperm donor that a lesbian can have a child. And the child adopted by a homosexual couple has a genealogical and a social origin.

In legalizing these new forms of family, Western societies give them a legitimate social existence, but that does not mean that public opinion is not still divided on the question.

Isn't there another apparently more innocuous legal development that marks a major turning point? I'm talking about making divorce easier.

Yes. The movement that most deeply alters parenthood and thus the Western system of kinship, inherited from centuries of Christianity or more recently from decades of the bourgeois family, is the fact that the couple no longer makes a family, that marriage is no longer a necessary condition for uniting to make a family, that alongside marriage there are all manner of cohabitation arrangements. But most of all, the dynamic created by the conjunction of two freedoms has a profound impact on the Western family. The first freedom is that, increasingly in the West, people marry for love, for affection. For centuries it was the families that married their children; today, children, having become adults, choose the partner with whom they will spend a part of their life for reasons that are more affective than material or social. This freedom to choose one's partner is completed by the freedom to dissolve the union when one or both partners no longer wish to live together. This freedom was granted by the state when it legalized divorce by mutual consent (in 1975 in France).

This conjunction of two freedoms, which opens the way to personal fulfilment, means that today, nearly

40 per cent of couples separate after seven to ten years. Which shows that love is a passion that sometimes fails to withstand the test of time. Today, it is unusual in our societies to find couples celebrating fifty or sixty years of marriage, their golden or diamond wedding anniversaries. With these liberties in place, now a man or a woman can divorce or separate several times over the course of their life, each time with the possibility to create a new family. The moral, religious and economic constraints that in preceding centuries locked individuals into the family they had founded for life have exploded. A change is settling in and spreading through our societies: the relations between parents and children in so-called re-composed or blended families. For if someone separates in order to live a new love, taking with them two children from their first couple, and the new partner also has children, what becomes of these children? For the adults, theirs was a conscious, free choice and new happiness. But the flip side of their love is that the children are forced to create relations with strangers who have become their quasi-father and quasi-mother or their quasi-brothers and -sisters. The adults' freedom and happiness thus necessarily have consequences for the subjective emotional and therefore personal development of their children.

The incest related by Camille Kouchner in *La Familia grande* (Le Seuil, 2021) concerns not a father and his son, but a stepfather, Olivier Duhamel and his stepson. Is this the sign that Western societies have extended the prohibition on incest to social kin created by remarriage?

The recognition that social parents play a fundamental role in societies arises spontaneously in our own. In a marriage where a woman or a man brings their children from an earlier marriage, popular opinion considers that the spouses should act 'like a mother and a father'; in other words, offer the children protection, education and affection, and provide their material conditions of existence and development, as though they were the mother and father who had engendered these children. Thus we often hear a man or a woman say: *My real father is the one who raised me, not the other one.* In the case of *La Familia grande*, the stepfather did not behave like a father: he used his situation as quasi-father to have sexual relations with his companion's son, thereby committing homosexual incest.

In France, parents from a second marriage were traditionally called *parâtre* and *marâtre*. These terms, which were negatively loaded from a sociological standpoint, were replaced by *beau-père* and *belle-mère*, affinal terms that in fact designate a fictional consanguinity. English distinguishes between *father-in-law* (alliance) and *stepfather* (a second marriage). The first and second husbands of a woman bear the same responsibilities to the children. The British *Children Act* (1989) stipulates that they share the duty to provide all children in the family with protection and to meet their physical, emotional, moral and educational needs. In France, there is a legal vacuum in this domain.

In speaking about *La Familia grande*, you talked about 'homosexual' incest. Does the incest taboo concern this form of sexuality as well?

Yes, it concerns homosexual relations as well, since human sexuality is both homo- and heterosexual. Many societies either deny the existence of homosexuality or condemn it as unnatural. But many others recognize it: these societies, which give homosexuality an important place in their construction and reproduction, also make it a component of their major political-religious initiations.

In Antiquity, for instance, it seems that the noble women of Lesbos, who were lesbians during their initiations, later conceived and bore children, which enabled the society to continue; these women were therefore recognized as being bisexual. In Oceania, it is frequent that male initiations require boys or young men to have homosexual relations with each other, at least until the time of their marriage; afterwards it is forbidden. However, there is a big difference between this ritual homosexuality imposed on one and all and homo-sexuality as a form of love for the other and a lifestyle, as found in Western societies.

Coming back to the new freedoms, do you think they're now secure?

This spiral of freedoms and their consequences is a social process that shows no sign of stopping. And that is because individual freedom of choice is a funda-mental value in Western societies. As our societies continually expand the field of individual freedoms, they must, at the same time, expand and define a new field of responsibilities, both for individuals enjoying ever greater freedom and for the state. The latter already plays this role since it guarantees by law that a child born out of wedlock has the same rights as a child born in wedlock; and it imposes the legal and moral obligation on adults who divorce or separate to fulfil their responsibilities to the children they have conceived, and to do so until the children's majority.

Needless to say, experience has shown that thousands of men who divorce forget to pay the child support they owe their wife who is raising their children; however, it sometimes also happens that women leave their husband and children for another life and forget their obligations.

Thus, Western societies are experiencing a combination of two transformations. On the one hand, the axis of alliance, one of the two fundamental pillars of kinship, is increasingly opening up to new forms of union (for example, same-sex). On the other hand, meanwhile, the descent axis is growing more complex, with the new ways of making children, and increasingly differentiating into diverging lines leading from an individual through successive unions and breakdowns to other unions and breakdowns that can split and fragment at any time.

This succession of coupling and uncoupling in monogamous societies gives rise to a sort of serial monogamy, which is in fact a successive polygamy, on the part of both men and women. These transformations are irreversible because they deeply correspond to the structures that constitute liberal capitalist societies. Such societies are liberal because they enshrine the principle, proclaimed by the French Revolution, of individual liberty and self-determination of peoples.

They are capitalistic because their economic system is based on capitalism, and we know that capitalism promotes personal success, individual success, risk-taking and so on.

Left to their own devices, these profound trans-formations, piling freedom upon freedom, increasingly call for the expansion and definition of the responsi-bilities not only of the individuals who live out and practise these freedoms, but of the state, which in each society is the source of the laws that enable us to live together. I would say that in Western societies, and in spite of resistances that were to be expected and are therefore normal (such as Poland), the Christian family model is on its way out, after having lasted for centu-ries and having been partially secularized through integration in the civil code by the bourgeoisie that replaced the aristocracies. That is what is the most affected, and which diminishes the social importance, notwithstanding its continued priority, of individuals' genealogical reference. Alternatively, the social kinship ties between individuals are expanding.

The same desire to choose one's partner freely and to advance in one's life also shows up strongly in the Muslim world, in Narendra Modi's India and in Xi Jinping's China. But in order to talk about process, we need first to begin by describing it and analysing the evolution of kinship relations in the rest of the world. Such is not my intention here, however.

In conclusion, we must by no means forget that, although kinship relations are changing in the West or elsewhere, nowhere are they the foundation of societies, and they are changing everywhere because societies change. And they change for reasons that, generally speaking, have nothing to do with kinship.

Conclusion

As an anthropologist, do you think, as many philosophers or clerics claim, that societies are based on family and kinship?

There is no such thing as kin-based societies, and there never has been, despite what all too many anthropologists and philosophers continue to affirm when talking about what used to be called 'primitive' societies. All individuals begin life in a restricted or extended kin group. This starting point is vital for their survival: it confers the initial identity. But, afterwards, as individuals develop, they become more than what they were at the outset: they are incorporated into the complexity of their society and of the era in which they live. When we compare societies, as anthropologists do, it is clear that nowhere does a society exist that is based on kinship.

What makes a society is the fact that social groups, whatever their nature – orders, castes, classes and so on – claim in common their *sovereignty* over a territory, its resources and its inhabitants. The social relations that create a form of sovereignty needed to make a society are political and religious in nature, and they are broader than kinship relations and groups, which they incorporate into their functioning. For thousands of years, it was only political-religious relations that enabled the formation of societies, which then went on to reproduce themselves, consciously, as a whole. Only in modern times did the evolution of certain societies lead to the separation between religion and the state, and to the affirmation of the people's sovereignty over their own destiny.

In every society, kinship relations find themselves subordinated to social relations, which encompass them, permeate them and at the same time cause them to evolve. But transformations in kinship relations and in the system characterizing them always engender another kinship system, and *nothing else*.

Before we separate, I would like one last time, as an anthropologist, to leave Western society and visit the kingdom of Tonga, which comprises 169 islands located in the middle of the Pacific Ocean. Tonga was one of the most stratified Polynesian societies, along with Hawaii and Tahiti. The society was divided into the body of commoners and an ethnic aristocracy, which ultimately derived its authority from the person of the paramount chief, the Tu'i Tonga. Each noble had a title giving him authority over a portion of the island territory and the people living there. The first European observers, at the end of the eighteenth century, reported that this society had two representations of the way babies are made, and that this duality corresponded to transformations in political power within the kingdom.

According to the first theory, and probably the oldest, the man made the child's bones from his sperm, while the woman made its flesh and blood from her menstrual blood. Thus, a clot of blood changed into a foetus, and then a soul took possession of the foetus; this, according to Tongans, was a gift from the ancestors or the gods to the living. In this model, the father and the mother were indeed the child's genitors, but once again, their action did not suffice to make the child, since, in the end, it was always a gift from the ancestors or the gods.

But there was a second model, according to which the child's whole substance came from the mother, while the only thing the man's sperm did was to block the menstrual blood in the woman's uterus. How then do they explain the transformation of the maternal blood clot into an embryo that will become a child?

According to this new explanation of the way a baby is made, the man as genitor disappears, becoming merely the one who prepares the woman for fecundation by a god or a man-god, the Tu'i Tonga. The Tu'i Tonga is thus credited with the god-like power to impregnate the woman with a fecundating breath, fruit of his dematerialized seed. In this second version, the woman's blood now makes the child's entire substance. We might think that, even more than the first model, the second glorifies women's procreative powers, but in fact it ultimately excludes male commoners entirely from the process of making their own children.

The origin of this second explanation seems to be connected to profound mutations that had occurred in the Tongan political system. Before the arrival of Europeans, the kinship relations existing between chiefly lines and the rest of the population had increasingly yielded to master–subject relations as the nobility concentrated its power over rights to land, labour, services and finally the very life of the rest of the population. These powers now separated the aristocracy definitively from the common people and in the imaginary of society raised nobles above commoners, bringing them closer to the gods and finally allowing them to claim the gods as direct ancestors.

The Tu'i Tonga, paramount chief, claimed in effect to descend from the union between a high Polynesian god (Tangaloa) and a human noblewoman, which was said to have resulted in the birth of the ancestor of the Tu'i Tonga's line. In turn, the Tu'i Tonga, in setting himself up as the fecundator of all women (without actually inseminating them) and as the fertilizer of all of the lands (without actually working them), became the father of all Tongans, their sole ancestor, such that all were thereafter related to the gods through him.

The example of the kingdom of Tonga shows, once again, that the domain of political-ritual relations over-spills the sphere of kinship relations while permeating them and manipulating them in its service. It is inter-esting that the Tu'i Tonga presented himself both as the chief and as the father (*tamai*) of all Tongans. The vocabulary of kinship, its images and its values were thus co-opted to symbolize and represent power.

In Ancient China, the emperor was known as the 'Unique Man', the only one capable of connecting Heaven and Earth and the people to his own ancestors and to the gods. Every year he was the first to perform the rites and sacrifices addressed to Heaven so that work on the land could begin and would produce a generous harvest that would bring prosperity to the population.

But, to return to the West, we cannot forget that, in the twentieth century, a bloody, bloodthirsty dictator, Joseph Stalin, was ironically but affectionately called 'the little father of the peoples' by his worshippers.

A Short Bibliography

Books

Augustine, Saint, 1972. *The City of God*. Translated by Henry Bettenson. New York and London, Penguin Classics.

Barry, Laurent, 2008. *La Parenté*. Paris, Gallimard.

Benveniste, Émile, 1973 (1969). *Indo-European Language and Society*. Translated by Elizabeth Palmer. London, Faber.

Bonte, Pierre (ed.), 1994. *Épouser au plus proche*. Paris, École des hautes études en sciences sociales.

Cai Hua, 1997. *Une Société sans père ni mari. Les Na de Chine*. Paris, Presses universitaires de France.

Chiland, Colette, 2003. *Le Transsexualisme*. Paris, Presses universitaires de France.

Dover, K. J., 1989. *Greek Homosexuality*. New York, Harvard Editions.

Dubreuil, Eric, 1998. *Des Parents de même sexe*. Paris, Odile Jacob.

Edwards, J., S. Franklin, E. Hirsch, F. Price and M. Strathern, 1992. *Technologies of Procreation: Kinship in the Age of Assisted Conception*. Manchester University Press.

Éribon, Didier, 2003. *Dictionnaire des cultures gays et lesbiennes*. Paris, Larousse.

Fine, Agnès (ed.), 1998. *Adoptions. Ethnologie des parentés choisies*. Paris, Éditions de la Maison des sciences de l'homme.

Fortes, Meier, 1983. *Rules and the Emergence of Society*. London, Royal Anthropological Institute of Great Britain.

Freud, Sigmund, 2001 (1913). *Totem and Taboo*. Translated by James Strachey. London and New York, Routledge.

Godelier, Maurice, 1983. *The Development of the Family and Marriage in Europe*. London, Cambridge University Press.

Godelier, Maurice, 2019. *Les Fondamentaux de la vie sociale*. Paris, CNRS Éditions.

Godelier, Maurice, 2020 (2004). *Metamorphoses of Kinship*. Translated by Nora Scott. London and New York, Verso.

Godelier, Maurice, T. Trautman and Tshon Sie Fat (eds), 1998. *Transformations of Kinship*. Washington, DC, Smithsonian Institution Press.

Goudsblom, Johan, 1992. *Fire and Civilization*. London, Penguin Books.

Gross, Martine, 2003. *L'Homoparentalité*. Paris, Presses universitaires de France.

Herdt, Gilbert, 1984. *Ritualized Homosexuality in Melanesia*. Berkeley, University of California Press.

Heritier, Françoise, 1981. *L'Exercice de la parenté*. Paris, Le Seuil.

Koran, 'The Quranic Corpus'. Translated by Mohsin Khan, quran-archive.org/the-quranic-corpus.

Lévi-Strauss, Claude, 1969 (1949). *The Elementary Structures of Kinship*. Translated by James Harle Bell, John Richard Von Sturmer and Rodney Needham. Boston, Beacon Press.

Lévi-Strauss, Claude, 2013 (2011). *The Other Face of the Moon*. Translated by Jane Marie Todd. Cambridge, MA, Belknap Press.

Levine, Nancy E., 1988. *The Dynamics of Polyandry*. Chicago, University of Chicago Press.

Lewin, Ellen, 1993. *Lesbian Mothers: Accounts of Gender in American Culture*. Ithaca, NY, Cornell University Press.

Malinowski, Bronisław, 1927. *The Father in Primitive Psychology*. New York, Norton Library.

Malinowski, Bronisław, 2003 (1927). *Sex and Repression in Savage Society*. New York, Routledge.

Ragone, Helena, 1994. *Surrogate Motherhood: Conception in the Heart*. New York, Boulder.

Sergent, Bernard, 1986. *L'Homosexualité initiatique dans l'Europe ancienne*. Paris, Payot.

Théry, Irène, 1999. *Le Démariage. Justice et vie privée*. Paris, Odile Jacob.

Vernier, Bernard, 2009. *La Prohibition de l'inceste*. Paris, L'Harmattan.

Weston, Kath, 1991. *Families We Choose: Lesbians, Gays, Kinship*. New York, Columbia University Press.

Articles

Belo, Jane, 1970. 'A Study of Customs Pertaining to Twins in Bali', in J. Belo, *Traditional Balinese Culture*. New York, Columbia University Press, pp. 3–56.

Bixler, Ray H., 1982. 'Sibling Incest in the Royal Families in Egypt, Peru and Hawaii', *Journal of Sex Research*, vol. 18, no. 3, pp. 264–81.

Bonnet, Doris, 1981. 'Le Retour de l'ancêtre', *Journal des africanistes*, vol. 51, pp. 149–82.

Cerny, Jaroslav, 1954. 'Consanguineous Marriages in Pharaonic Egypt', *Journal of Egyptian Archaeology*, vol. 40, pp. 23–9.

Cohen, David, 1987. 'Law, Society and Homosexuality in Classical Athens', *Past and Present*, no. 117, pp. 3–21.

Deputte, Bertrand L., 1985. 'L'Evitement de l'inceste chez les primates non-humains', *Nouvelle Revue d'ethnopsychiatrie*, no. 3, pp. 41–72.

Diemberger, Hildegard, 1993. 'Blood, Sperm and the Mountain', in T. del Valle (ed.), *Gendered Anthropology*. London, Routlege and Kegan, pp. 8–127.

Diemberger, Hildegard, 1998. 'Montagnes sacrées, os des ancêtres, sang maternel au Népal', in M. Godelier and M. Panoff (eds), *La Production du corps*. Paris, Éditions des Archives contemporaines, pp. 269–80.

Douaire-Marsaudon, Françoise, 2002. 'Le Bain mystérieux de la Tu'i Tonga fefine. Germanité, inceste et mariage sacré en Polynésie', *Anthropos*, vol. 97, pp. 147–62, 519–28.

Geertz, Clifford, 2001. 'The Visit. Review of a Society without Fathers or Husbands: The Na of China, by Cai Hua', *New York Review of Books*, 18 October.

Golombok, Susan, 1983. 'Children in Lesbian and Single-Parent Households', *Journal of Child Psychology and Psychiatry*, no. 24, pp. 551–72.

Goody, Jack, 1956. 'A Comparative Approach to Incest and Adultery', *British Journal of Sociology*, vol. 7, pp. 286–305.

Gough, Kathleen, 1952. 'A Comparison of Incest Prohibitions and Rules of Exogamy in Three Matrilineal Groups of the Malabar Coast', *International Archives of Ethnography*, no. 46, pp. 81–105.

Greene, Beth, 1988. 'The Institution of Woman-Marriage in Africa: A Cross-Cultural Analysis', *Ethnology*, vol. 37, no. 4, pp. 395–412.

Herrenschmidt, Clarisse, 1994. 'Le Xwêtôdas ou "mariage incestueux" en Iran ancien', in P. Bonte (ed.), *Épouser au plus proche. Inceste, prohibition et stratégies matrimoniales autour de la Méditerranée*. Paris, École des hautes études en sciences sociales, pp. 113–25.

Hopkins, Keith, 1980. 'Brother-Sister Marriage in Roman Egypt', *Comparative Studies in Society and History*, no. 22, pp. 303–54.

Isaac, Glynn, 1978. 'Food Sharing and Human Evolution: African Evidence from the Plio-Pleistocene of East Africa', *Journal of Anthropological Research*, vol. 34, pp. 311–25.

James, Steve R., 1989. 'Humanoid Use of Fire in the Lower and Middle Pleistocene', *Current Anthropology*, vol. 30, pp. 1–26.

Knauft, Bruce, 1987. 'Homosexuality in Melanesia', *Journal of Psychoanalytic Anthropology*, vol. 10, no. 2, pp. 155–91.

Lallemand, Suzanne, 1988. 'Adoption, fosterage et alliance', *Anthropologie et sociétés*, vol. 12, no. 2, pp. 25–40.

Levine, Hal B., 2003. 'Gestational Surrogacy: Nature and Culture in Kinship', *Ethnology*, vol. 42, no. 3, pp. 173–86.

Mead, Margaret, 1968. 'Incest', in *International Encyclopedia of the Social Sciences*. New York, Macmillan, vol. 7, pp. 115–22.

Mehlman, Patrick, 1988. 'L'Evolution des soins paternels chez les primates et les hominidés', *Anthropologie et sociétés*, vol. 12, no. 3, pp. 131–49.

Monberg, Torben, 1975. 'Fathers Were Not Genitors', *Man*, vol. 10, no. 1, pp. 34–40.

Moore, J., and R. Ali, 1984. 'Are Dispersal and Inbreeding Avoidance Related?', *Animal Behaviour*, no. 32, pp. 94–112.

Ronen, Avraham, 1998. 'Domestic Fire as Evidence for Language', in T. Akazawa (ed.), *Neandertals and Modern Humans in Western Africa*. New York, Plenum Press, pp. 439–47.

Schneider, David M., 1976. 'The Meaning of Incest', *Journal of the Polynesian Society*, vol. 85, no. 2, pp. 149–69.

Tonkinson, Robert, 1978. 'Semen versus Spirit-Child in a Western Desert Culture', in L. R. Hiatt (ed.),

Australian Aboriginal Concepts. Atlantic Highlands, NJ, Humanities Press, pp. 81–90.

Vidal, Jean-Marie, 1985. 'Explications biologiques et anthropologiques de l'interdit de l'inceste', *Nouvelle Revue d'ethnopsychiatrie*, no. 3, pp. 75–107.

Waal, Frans De, 1989. 'La Réconciliation chez les primates', *La Recherche*, no. 210, pp. 592–610.

Waal, Frans De, 1993. 'Bonobo Sex and Society', *Scientific American*, March, pp. 58–64.